WELCOME TO FRENCH
with SESAME STREET

J. P. PRESS

Lerner Publications ◆ Minneapolis

Dear Parents and Educators,

From its very beginning, *Sesame Street* has promoted mutual respect and cultural understanding by featuring a cast of diverse and lovable characters. *Welcome to French* introduces children to the wonderful, wide world we live in. In this book *Sesame Street* friends present handy and fun vocabulary in a language kids may not know. These words can help young readers welcome new friends. Have fun as you explore!

Sincerely,

The Editors at Sesame Workshop

Table of Contents

WELCOME!

Bienvenue!
(Say bee-ehn-ven-OOH)

How to Speak French!

Practice speaking French! Each word is broken up into separate sounds called syllables. Do you see the syllable in CAPITAL LETTERS? That's the sound that you emphasize the most!

Hello.
Bonjour.
bon-JOOR

Meet Georges.
He lives in France.

What is your name?
Comment tu t'appelles?
koh-MOH too tah-pell

My name is . . .
Je m'appelle . . .
juh mah-PEHLL . . .

Je m'appelle Abby.

Will you be my friend?
Veux-tu être mon amie?
vuh TOO eh-tre mone
ah-MEE

friendship
amitié
ah-mee-tee-AY

**best
friends**

**meilleurs
amis**

**may-URS
ah-MEE**

This is
my family!
Voilà, c'est
ma famille!

dad
papa
pah-PA

mom
maman
mah-MA

brother
frère
frair

sister
sœur
seure

grandma
grand-mère
grahn-MAIR

grandpa
grand-père
grahn-PAIR

Thank you.
Merci.
mair-SEE

You are welcome.
De rien.
duh ree-AIN

Please.
S'il vous plaît.
seel voo PLAY

I'm sorry.
Je suis désolé.
juh SWEE
day-so-LAY

13

breakfast
petit déjeuner
puh-TEE day-
juh-NAY

lunch
déjeuner
day-juh-NAY

dinner
dîner
dee-NAY

hungry
affamé
ah-fah-MAY

thirsty
assoiffé
ah-swa-FAY

Cookie Monster wants a snack.

Cookie Monster veut une collation.

How are you?
Comment allez-vous?
koh-MOH tal-AY-voo

I'm fine, thank you.
Bien, merci.
bee-EHN mair-SEE

This is Griotte.
She's from France.

I like you.
Je t'aime.
juh TEM

happy
heureux
heu-REU

grumpy
grincheux
grain-SHEU

proud
fier
fee-AIR

excited
enthousiaste
ehn-thoo-see-AH-ste

dog
chien
SHE-eh

fish
poisson
pwa-SOH

bird
oiseau
wah-ZO

cat
chat
sha

animals
animaux
ah-nee-MO

colors

couleurs

coo-LEHR

My favorite color is . . .

Ma couleur préférée est . . .

mah coo-LEHR pray-fay-RAY ay . . .

red
rouge
roo-je

orange
orange
oh-rhan-JE

yellow
jaune
JHO-ne

green
vert
vair

blue
bleu
bluh

purple
violet
vee-oh-LAY

Let's play!
On va jouer!
ohn vah joo-AY

toys
jouets
joo-AY

I like to paint.
J'aime peindre.

Goodbye.
Au revoir.
oh re-VWAR

See you soon!
À bientôt !
AH bee-ehn-TOE

Count It!

1 one **un** uhn

2 two **deux** deuh

3 three **trois** twah

4
four
quatre
CAT-re

7
seven
sept
set

5
five
cinq
sank

8
eight
huit
weet

6
six
six
seeseh

9
nine
neuf
nuhf

10
ten
dix
deese

Abby's Favorite Words

magic
magique
mah-JICK

magic wand
baguette magique
bah-GET mah-JICK

fairy
fée
faye

Further Information

BBC Primary Languages: French
http://www.bbc.co.uk/schools/primarylanguages/french

Learn French
https://www.youtube.com/watch?v=3bvDIbMaBsA

Oui Love Books. *Oui Love Sports: An English/French Word Book*. Chicago: Odéon Livre, 2018.

Parkes, Elle. *Let's Explore France*. Minneapolis: Lerner Publications, 2018.

Sesame Street
http://www.sesamestreet.org

Lerner Publications Company
An imprint of Lerner Publishing Group, Inc.
241 First Avenue North
Minneapolis, MN 55401 USA

For reading levels and more information, look up this title at www.lernerbooks.com.

Main body text set in Mikado.
Typeface provided by HVD Fonts.

Additional image credits: ESB Professional/Shutterstock.com, p. 20 (dog); clarst5/Shutterstock.com, p. 20 (bird); Eric Isselee/Shutterstock.com, p. 20 (cat); Gunnar Pippel/Shutterstock.com, p. 20 (fish); Super Prin/Shutterstock.com, p. 23 (butterfly); Tiplyashina Evgeniya/Shutterstock.com, p. 25 (easel); irin-k/Shutterstock.com, pp. 28, 29 (ladybug).

Library of Congress Cataloging-in-Publication Data

Names: Press, J. P., 1993– author. | Children's Television Workshop, contributor.
Title: Welcome to French with Sesame Street / J. P. Press.
Other titles: Sesame Street (Television program)
Description: Minneapolis : Lerner Publications, 2019. | Series: Sesame Street welcoming words | Includes bibliographical references.
Identifiers: LCCN 2018059485 (print) | LCCN 2019007810 (ebook) | ISBN 9781541562486 (eb pdf) | ISBN 9781541554986 (lb : alk. paper) | ISBN 9781541574939 (pb : alk. paper)
Subjects: LCSH: French language—Conversation and phrase books—English—Juvenile literature.
Classification: LCC PC2121 (ebook) | LCC PC2121 .P87 2019 (print) | DDC 448.3/421—dc23

LC record available at https://lccn.loc.gov/2018059485

Manufactured in the United States of America
1-45821-42698-3/7/2019